ANNE BAILEY

Frontier Scout

ANNE BAILEY

Frontier Scout

Mary R. Furbee

MORGAN
REYNOLDS
Publishers, Inc.

620 South Elm Street Suite 223
Greensboro, North Carolina 27406
http://www.morganreynolds.com

ANNE BAILEY: FRONTIER SCOUT

Cover image courtesy of North Wind Picture Archives

Library of Congress Cataloging-in-Publication Data

Furbee, Mary R. (Mary Rodd), 1954-
    Anne Bailey : frontier scout / Mary R. Furbee.
        p. cm.
    Includes bibliographical references (p.) and index.
    ISBN 1-883846-70-6
    1. Bailey, Anne Hennis, 1742-1825--Juvenile literature. 2. Women pioneers--West
Virginia--Biography--Juvenile literature. 3. Pioneers--West
Virginia--Biography--Juvenile literature. 4. Frontier and pioneer life--West
Virginia--Kanawha River Valley--Juvenile literature. 5. Kanawha River Valley (W.
Va.)--History--Juvenile literature. 6. Kanawha River Valley (W.
Va.)--Biography--Juvenile literature. [1. Bailey, Anne Hennis, 1742-1825. 2. Pioneers. 3.
Women--Biography. 4. Frontier and pioneer life--West Virginia.] I. Title.

F241.B15 F87 2001
975.4'303'092--dc21
[B]

                                                                        00-054904

Printed in the United States of America
First Edition

For Mike, my best friend

Contents

An eighteenth century woodcut of Anne Bailey.

Prologue

In 1772, a thirty-two-year-old widow from western Virginia took off her worn petticoat. From a peg on the wall of her small log cabin, she took down a fringed buckskin jacket and pants. She put on the rough leather clothes, tucked a tomahawk into her belt, and hefted a long musket rifle. She stepped out of her cabin, mounted her horse, and rode west to become the only known female frontier scout during the American Revolution.

Fifty years later, as an old woman, the former scout told stories about her adventures. After she died, the tales spread and changed. Over time they grew as tangled and twisted as the red-berried bittersweet vine of the Alleghenies. Not much time passed before the real woman—Anne Hennis Trotter Bailey—was transformed into the mythic, invincible "Mad Anne Bailey."

The "Mad Anne Bailey" legends never spread as far and wide as those told about other scouts—coonskin-cap-wearing Daniel Boone and Davy Crocket, for example. History tends to focus on leading citizens, which both Crocket and Boone became in their later years. Anne Bailey never joined these respectable ranks.

Not all the "Mad Anne" legends are flattering. Some storytellers did not think much of a woman who did a "man's job." They called her a "mongrel with long matted hair," who drank whiskey like water and "pulled from her blouse Indian scalps dripping with blood." More sympathetic storytellers called her a homespun hero and "the original Girl Scout." In an epic poem, a Civil War soldier painted a heroic picture of "an army saved by a gentle woman."

These legends are wonderful stories, and a few of them are included at the back of this book. But in the chapters that follow, you will find the true story of Anne's ordinary, yet extraordinary, life.

Anne Bailey was an indentured servant, pioneer homesteader, daughter, wife, and widow. She also was a rebel who became a free and independent woman—just as the American colonies became a free and independent nation.

Chapter One

"Bound" for America

Anne Hennis, nineteen years old, tramped through ruts carved into the mud by the jumble of farm wagons, ox carts, coaches, and carriages crowding the narrow streets of Liverpool, England. Anne hurried toward the docks at Old Pool, where she would board a ship bound for the American colonies. The year was 1761.

The streets that Anne rushed through were crowded with brick and wooden warehouses. Around her, laborers bent low under heavy sacks of raw cotton tied to their backs or pushed carts loaded with pottery snuffboxes painted by workmen for a farthing each. Weavers brought bolts of woolen cloth woven from American cotton. Coopers hammered wooden barrels used to store the sugar, tea, and coffee that were brought in great sailing ships from the West Indian colonies.

Anne squeezed past a rowdy crowd of newsboys, lamplighters, tradesmen, and gentlemen gathered around a pair of fighting roosters. Wagons tore through the street at breakneck speed. Stagecoaches sagged under the weight of passengers riding on the roofs and bumpers, like baby monkeys clinging to their mothers' backs. In the shadows of warehouses and peddlers' stalls, ragged urchins begged from passersby. They grubbed in the muck for coins tossed from the windows of gold-trimmed ebony carriages.

Anne barely stood five feet tall, but she was solid and strong. A long cape covered her cotton gown, the laced bodice worn thin with wear. A straw bonnet tied with ribbons kept the fog from her wide, round face. Between strong cheekbones, her green eyes were flecked with brown, like ripe pears in autumn.

A young woman of the servant class, Anne had lived her entire life in this melting-pot city of Irish, Welsh, and English people. Every year, the city swelled in size as poor people who had been evicted from tenant farms came to Liverpool looking for work. But jobs were scarce and wages were low. Taxes were high and crime was common. In crumbling slums and along mean little alleyways, the poor crowded from basement to attic into cold, cramped houses. The smell of

Anne Hennis boarded a ship bound for America at the port of Liverpool, England.

dead animals and open sewer drains filled the air. Outside taverns and alehouses, women stood guard to prevent their husbands from gambling or drinking away their wages. The prisons were filled with people jailed for stealing bread. The poor often died young, as Anne's parents had.

Liverpool was no place for an uneducated working girl to build a good life. Anne decided to work as an indentured servant in the American colonies. The Bell family paid her passage to Virginia, one of Britain's thirteen American colonies. In exchange, Anne agreed to work for them for four years without pay. Anne would call them master and mistress, and they would call her "the bound girl." After four years of working for the Bells, Anne would have her freedom. Her master would also give her fifty acres of land, an axe, two hoes, and a dress. If she married, all her property would be turned over to her husband, for that was the law in both England and the American colonies.

Ever since Anne was a small child, Liverpool had buzzed with talk of the American colonies. People said wolves, wildcats, and red savages with scalping knives terrorized the "God-fearing" colonists. But people also said that wheat and corn practically planted themselves, and pigs walked the street asking: "Would you like some meat to eat?" People said that in the colonies, even a street sweeper could become as rich as the King himself. In Britain, only the upper classes and merchants were rich, owned land, and ate meat.

Anne, however, did not dream of wealth. She dreamed instead of living a free life with a husband of her own. People said there were ten men for every woman in the New World. She would marry a free man, perhaps a soldier like her father. With him she would build a good life.

Anne arrived at the wharf, where the black Mersey River meets the green Irish Sea. She pushed past clusters of sweaty sailors and shackled slaves. She darted around men in powdered wigs and three-cornered hats. She skirted beggars in rags and ladies in low-cut gowns and wide hooped skirts. Rainbow-colored feather plumes sprouted from their foot-high hairdos, quivering in the damp, heavy air.

As Anne climbed the ramp to her ship, her strong shoulders pitched forward under the load of her belongings. Strands of long auburn hair blew about her lightly freckled cheeks. The three tall sails of the ship unfurled as it moved out onto the Irish Sea, flapping and flurrying like sheets on a line. The sweat chilled on Anne's body, as if she faced a winter wind.

Standing on the crowded deck with the other passengers, Anne looked back at the land of her birth. She remembered the sickness and hunger. She remembered her parents' recent deaths. She recalled a visit to London when she was five years old. Her father had taken her to see the red-hatted Beefeater guards who marched in front of the turreted Tower of London. Anne and her father had stood in a cheering crowd of thousands and watched the execution of Lord Lovat, "the Traitor." Anne's father said Lovat had been convicted of joining the Scottish rebels against King George II. Sitting on her father's broad shoulders,

Anne shuddered as the black-hooded executioner swung the giant axe onto the fallen Lord's neck. This was the only execution Anne ever saw, but her father told her many stories of royal feuds, bloody battles, and heroic deaths.

Anne did not dwell on the past for long. As England's shores faded away, the crew herded her and 300 other indentured servants bound for the American colonies into the ship's dark hold. Anne dreamed of a better future in a bountiful land.

Holding onto good thoughts was hard in the ship's stinking, rocking hold. Anne and 300 other servants lived and slept there crammed together like fish in a barrel. The ship pitched about in terrifying storms. A sour smell of wet wood, fermenting ale, and spoiled food forced Anne to hold her skirt to her nose. As time passed, food rations of stale biscuits and wormy beef grew meager. Some passengers trapped and ate the ship's rats and mice to survive. Many passengers grew seasick. Others caught illnesses from the rotten food, hunger, and filth. Some died, including many children. Family members cried and prayed as the sailors dropped the bodies overboard.

Healthy and strong, Anne survived. On clear days, the captain sometimes allowed the passengers to come up on deck for a while. Anne breathed the sea air and let the wind blow through her hair. She watched dolphins dance on their tails in the ship's wake and screeching gulls dive for fish. She searched the horizon for ships, praying they would not meet up with any of the notorious pirates who terrorized the Atlantic.

After several weeks on the wind-tossed ocean, the ship reached the Cape of Virginia. It passed Smith's Island and sailed thirty-five miles up the wide James River. The ship dropped anchor in Jamestown. Sailors rowed to shore for fresh food. Anne and the others stuffed their hungry bellies that night. Anne liked her first taste of the homegrown food of the American colonies: corncakes, pigeon pie, cider, and ale.

As the James River lapped against the ship, thousands of tiny flashing lights appeared and a chorus of croaking echoed across the water. Anne marveled at the New World's small wonders: twinkling fireflies and bullfrogs as long as her own foot.

The next day, Anne watched as some servants were auctioned on the ship. The ship's captain sold them to get payment for their passage. Her face grew hard as parents were separated from children and husbands were separated from wives. Planters, merchants, and farmers bought some of the servants. Men called "soul

drivers" bought others to resell at country fairs. Anne was glad an agent had bought her in England especially for the Bells, for it spared her the humiliation of the auction block.

Chapter Two

Across the Blue Ridge

The next morning, Anne left the ship and boarded a flatboat headed up the James River. Perched on her sack of belongings, Anne watched the passing scenes of her new homeland. A million colonists now called Virginia home. By 1775, the population would more than double.

The riverboat passed the road to Williamsburg, with its neat cobblestone streets, colleges, newspapers, and dancing schools. Vast tobacco fields and lofty brick mansions surrounded by sweet-smelling magnolias, scarlet climbing roses, and manicured lawns lined the banks of the river. Clusters of slave log cabins, barns, stables, and blacksmith shops made each plantation look like a small village.

As the boat approached Richmond, Anne and the

other servants could not hear one another talk over the roar of the James River Falls. The boat docked, and a man standing next to a rough wooden wagon called out the names of the servants he was hired to deliver to their new masters in the Shenandoah Valley. When he shouted her name, "Anne Hennis," Anne climbed aboard the kind of rough ox-drawn cart that settlers had nicknamed "shakeguts."

The cart bumped and heaved along the James River Turnpike and across the Blue Ridge Mountains. As the wagon climbed the rolling hills, Anne marveled at the ghostly sycamores spreading their leafy branches across the road. The zigzag fences of split rails that rimmed the green tobacco fields and apple orchards looked like none she had ever seen in England.

Gradually, the hills grew steeper and the fields gave way to dense woodlands. The horses, sweating and snorting with the effort, led the cart over a steep rise. At the top of the hill, they stopped to rest. Anne drank cool water at a roadside spring. She stood on a boulder and looked out over a deep chasm in the earth. A wide plain stretched as far as her eyes could see. In the center wound a silver ribbon of river. Swaths of rippling golden wheat, green corn, and red clover surrounded the stone and log houses and barns. Plumes of gray

Anne crossed the James River on her way to her new home in the Shenandoah Valley.

smoke curled upward from farmhouse chimneys to meet swirling white clouds.

In the distance, far across the Valley, shadowy gray-green ridges jutted high into a sky as vast as the ocean Anne had just crossed. Indians claimed those western Allegheny ridges—part of the Appalachian range that spread from Maine to Georgia—as their hunting grounds. Only a handful of white trappers had ever ventured into their dark reaches. Never had Anne seen mountains so high and valleys so low. Looking into the distance, Anne could not know that someday she would call that dense western wilderness home.

Two months after she left Liverpool, Anne Hennis reached the Shenandoah Valley farm of Joseph and Elizabeth Bell. A few miles distant lay the village of

Staunton, with a dozen houses, log courthouse, trading post, water-powered sawmill, and a tavern.

Anne joined several hundred whites who had settled in the Shenandoah Valley over the past thirty years. Before them, the Delaware, Catawba, and Monocan Indians hunted and camped in the Valley. For thousands of years, the Indians had hunted buffalo, elk, bear, turkey, and deer and caught trout in the Shenandoah River. They called the river the "Daughter of the Stars." After the Great Spirit created the earth, the Indians said, the morning stars came together on the shores of a quiet silver lake. Beautiful blue mountains bordered the lake, and the stars lit the mountain tops with their robes of fire. The stars sang songs of joy and pledged to gather above the quiet waters every thousand years.

At first, Indians and whites lived in peace. But as the white population grew, hostilities escalated. Whites and Indians fought with rifle and tomahawk over who would leave and who would stay. The Indians killed many settlers and took many women and children captive. But white settlers soon outnumbered the Indians, and in the end, the native people retreated west into the Alleghenies.

Anne joined other servants and slaves at Joseph and

Elizabeth Bell's farmhouse. She worked twelve hours a day, six days a week—milking cows, stoking fires, threshing wheat, and spinning flax. She learned to make medicine from woodland plants—boneset for fever, willow bark for the head, pennyroyal for the stomach. She grew handy with an axe and a musket rifle. Mountain lions and wolves killed cows, sheep, and chickens, so everyone learned to shoot. The Colonial government offered a bounty for every wolf's head, and soon no wolves were left in the Valley.

Anne's only holiday was Sunday, which was set aside for prayer. She attended the Presbyterian Stone Church with the Bell family. The church was the pride of the community. The earliest Valley settlers had carved thick blocks from native stone and laid them on top of one another in neat rows. The women had loaded river sand on "drags" pulled by horses and mixed it with crushed limestone to make mortar. Anne stood in a separate section of the church for servants, listening to sermons so long that some people fainted from hunger and fatigue.

One memorable Sunday at Stone Church, Anne watched spellbound as Reverend Craig baptized a man named Selim from North Africa. A Valley hunter had found him in the woods starving and naked except for the bloody rags tied to his feet. He spoke a strange foreign language. The people of Stone Church cared for him, and he learned English. Then he told them he was the son of a wealthy man from Algeria, and he had been captured by a Spanish ship. The Spanish brought him to the Mississippi River and sold him to the Shawnee. Selim escaped and made his way to the Valley. The people of Stone Church believed his story because he knew several foreign languages and could read Reverend Craig's Greek Bible.

For thirty years, Scotch-Irish Presbyterians similar to the Bells had been settling in the Staunton, Virginia, area. After being driven out of Scotland by the Church of England, they fled to Ireland, where they clashed with the Catholic majority. Finally, they came to Virginia and found a place where they could worship freely.

The Bells owned thousands of acres of fertile farm-land and several servants and slaves. Yet they lived simply worked as hard as those who called them mistress and master. The English people east of the Blue Ridge thought the Scotch-Irish Valley people were inferior. Valley people said "quoth he" instead of "said he," so the Easterners called them "Cohees." The Valley people thought little of the Easterners, too.

They called them "Tuckahoes." Tuckahoe was the Indian name for a large, fat mushroom that grew underground.

Although Anne was English, she soon felt she belonged to the hardy Valley clan. People said the Presbyterians had such a fear of God that it left no room for fearing men, and Valley folk were known as fierce fighters. Even Tuckahoes, who felt superior to the western Virginians, counted on them to repel Indian attacks and to push westward into the wilderness that the Indians and French also claimed. The Valley people, they believed, would stand firm and fight to control the land.

In fact, many Valley men were gone to fight for the English far away in the west, along the Ohio River, when Anne arrived. They were fighting in a war that England had been waging against the French and Indians for land along the fertile Mississippi River. Anne's master, Joseph Bell, fought among them.

When England rose to victory in the French and Indian War in 1763, France gave up their claim to the land west of the Valley. The Valley people rejoiced—until King George III of England sent word that his subjects were not permitted to settle the land they had just won in battle. The King issued a royal proclamation saying that the land west of the Valley—from the Alleghenies to the Ohio River and beyond—belonged to the Indians. King George forbade his subjects to settle there. The seeds of rebellion against the English King were sown in the hearts of the mountaineers.

King George III was trying to stop the endless hostilities between white settlers and Indians. The King hoped to develop a profitable fur-trading relationship with the Indians, as the French had. But people in the Valley were cash-poor and land-hungry. The grown children of Valley farmers, new arrivals, and freed indentured servants were anxious toclaim the free and fertile land waiting for them in the western wilderness. The Indians—and the King—tried to stop the settlers.

Old-timers told Anne that the situation had not always been this way. At first, many white settlers were friendly with Indians and content to share the land. Ten years earlier, when Valley men had brutally murdered members of a tribe of peaceful Indians, many in the community became furious. From the pulpit of Stone Church, Reverend Craig condemned the killers and banished them from the church.

At the Bells, Anne often met visiting hunters and trappers who had adopted Indian ways and married

George III, ruled as King of England from 1760-1820.

Indian women. They defended the Indians. The woodsmen said whites had driven out the Indians' game, introduced them to alcohol, stolen their lands, and taught them their "ornery tricks." White settlers did not understand the relationship the Indians had with the land, the hunters said. The streams and rivers were more than just water to the Indians, they were the blood of their ancestors.

But the Bells and most of Anne's neighbors felt differently. They thought that God had led them to the Valley. After all, the Indians held no deeds to the land, built no schools, and worshipped "heathen" Gods. Many of the settlers also craved revenge against the Indians for relatives who had been killed and captured during the French and Indian War.

To most white settlers, including Anne, Indians were the enemy.

Chapter Three

Until Death Do Us Part

Each summer, Anne and the other servants joined hundreds of settlers, planters, soldiers, servants, and slaves for three days of merrymaking at the Staunton Fair. While farmers sold livestock and farm produce, store clerks gave girls hair ribbons called "fairings." Anne danced jigs, square sets, and reels on the dirt street in front of the big log courthouse. She gaped at tightrope walkers and a trained bear that danced and bellowed on command. She laughed and cheered as young men competed in obstacle races, boxing contests, and whistling matches. In one race, the young men chased a fat hog with a greased tail. The first to lift the hog off the ground by his tail and spin him around won. Prizes ranged from a new saddle or silver shoe buckles to plum pudding or tobacco.

Sandy-haired Richard Trotter looked like many men Anne met at the fair. His beard looked as rough and tangled as a brier bush, and his fringed leather jacket was trimmed with soft mink fur. He stood so tall he had to duck through the Bells' front door when he came courting. He had been a scout in the French and Indian War, and like Anne's father, told stories of adventure, ambush, and battle.

Richard told Anne how as a young boy in 1755, he had marched north with a unit of Virginia Provincials. The blue-coated Virginians joined General Braddock's Royal Redcoats, just arrived from England. They met in Cumberland and marched through Pennsylvania to the beat of a drum and the sprightly tune of a high-pitched penny whistle. The army neared French Fort Duquesne in Western Pennsylvania, when suddenly the French and Indians took them by surprise. Bullets came thick and fast from gullies and trees as the French and Indians shot down 800 of the 1,200 soldiers.

Richard's eyes darkened as he told Anne how General Braddock had not listened to the Virginians. They had warned Braddock not to march in neat squares, out in the open, as if they fought on an English battlefield. But the stubborn British general would not listen. The dead were mostly Royal forces, for the Virginians were quick and wily. Braddock himself died, and three bullets tore through the hat of the Virginia officer, Colonel George Washington, but he remained unharmed. Washington led Richard Trotter and the other Virginians through the forest, covering the Royal army's retreat over blood-soaked ground.

After the battle, Richard told Anne he had returned to the Valley to fight off a wave of Indian raids. To defend the region settlers built a long line of log forts along the foothills of the western mountains. Richard marched between the forts to keep watch, while remote settlers took refuge when hostile Indians came near. Sometimes, Richard told Anne, settlers did not reach the forts on time, and the Indians left paths of destruction. They took everything of value to them and

Richard Trotter kept watch between the western Virginian forts to protect other settlers from Indian raids.

destroyed the rest. Houses, barns, and crops were burned to ashes. Dishes, looms, and clothing lay torn and shattered on the scorched ground. Some settlers were scalped and killed; others were taken prisoner by the Indians.

The few isolated settlements deeper in the mountains fared the worst, Richard told Anne. People there were further from forts, and Indians had less trouble launching surprise attacks in isolated areas. Richard told Anne how, over in Draper's Meadow along the Greenbrier River, Mary Draper Ingles and her young sons were captured by the Shawnee. Mary's story had spread far and wide, for she had escaped and hiked home. The journey was 850 miles long and took Mary through New River Gorge—a 1,000 foot trench that even the Indians said was impassible. One of Mary's sons had died during his captivity, but her other son grew to manhood with the Indians. Years later, Mary's family paid the Indians a ransom for her surviving son. He had grown so accustomed to living with the Indians that he was not happy to rejoin white civilization, and he did not want to return.

Anne enjoyed Richard's stories. Richard liked Anne's broad smile, lively eyes, and plain-spoken ways. When the French and Indian War ended and Anne's term of service was finished, the young couple married. The Bells hosted a wedding feast for the newlyweds, inviting households for miles around. The table boasted beef, turkey, deer, bear, corn, and pumpkin pie. After dinner, the party-goers danced squares and jigs until dawn. When weary guests tried to catch a few winks in a quiet corner, other guests hunted them down. The slackers paraded on the floor and the fiddler was ordered to play "Hang Out till Tomorrow Morning." The next day, the weary young couple set out southward into the foothills of the Alleghenies to claim and tame a plot of land all their own.

The most valuable farmland was flat and bordered by rivers. But for his service in the French and Indian War, Richard had been given a remote hilltop claim, forty-five miles southwest of Staunton, just beyond the fertile valley in the foothills of the Appalachians. The natural grassy glen bordered the headwaters of 200-foot Falling Springs Waterfall. The small clearing yielded enough corn to survive, until more forest could be cut down. The woods around the clearing contained trees as wide as a Conestoga wagon. The woods drew beaver, deer, bear, and moose for meat and furs.

Sometimes a planter named Thomas Jefferson (who

later drafted the Declaration of Independence) brought friends from his home to the east to see Falling Springs Waterfall. Jefferson told his friends he was taking them to see "the only remarkable cascade in Augusta County."

Richard and Anne built a crude log cabin. They chopped down young oaks and laid them notch to saddle. As chips swirled in the air like dry leaves in an autumn windstorm, a smell resembling fermenting cider filled the air. The young couple filled the gaps between the logs with a sand and mud mixture and hung a thick maple door on wooden hinges. Over the door, a gallant set of buck's horns cradled a rust-colored rifle as long as Anne was tall. A frayed powder horn hung from the scuffed barrel.

On a rough plank loft in the rafters lay a mattress stuffed with dry leaves. In front of the fireplace, two three-legged stools were pulled up to a puncheon table made from a tree split in half. Coats and shirts hung from pegs on the walls. Instead of glass, their single window was made from paper oiled with bear grease, through which shone a honey-gold shaft of light.

Everyday, Anne and Richard cleared more ground for plowing. They grubbed saplings and thorny vines from around the clearing. They chopped "girdling"

Settlers in the frontier used the available resources to build their log cabins.

rings into the bark of huge gnarled tree trunks, which caused the old trees to soon die. Stripped of their bark and leafy branches, they resembled giant rain-washed skeletons reaching toward heaven. Around the giant trunks, Anne and Richard plowed crumbly black soil and seeded it with corn. In high, blazing fires that sent sparks flying into the black night, the young couple burned the branches and brush they had collected.

Richard hunted and skinned game, nailing the hides to the cabin walls. Years of scouting served him well as a trapper, for he knew the animals' lairs and haunts. At first, the couple pulled their own plow and hunted using only a "Shank's mare"—the term settlers had for their own two feet. Most settlers just starting out set traps and collected furs to trade for an ox or two to help with plowing, hauling, and other heavy work. But Anne and Richard had their hearts set on a horse. They traded their wares for a strong and sleek horse. They named the jet black gelding Liverpool, after Anne's hometown across the ocean. Anne braided cornhusks into ropes for hitching Liverpool to their simple wooden plow and cart.

Anne baked cornbread in the ashes of an open fire. She roasted venison on a spit, brewed tea from sassafras leaves, and made lye soap from ashes. She gathered fallen nuts from around the ground beneath a giant hickory, its scaly bark like the black-brown hairs of an old man's beard. In the evenings, Anne and Richard roasted the nuts in the embers of a dying fire. They listened to the night-wood's sounds—the wolves' howls, the panther's cries, the owl's mournful song.

Chapter Four

On Her Own Terms

Anne and Richard soon were expecting a child. When the birth pains began, Richard fetched Elizabeth Mann, a neighbor, to help. Then he took refuge by Falling Springs Waterfall where the roaring water drowned out Anne's groans and cries. Several hours later, Elizabeth fetched Richard. Anne lay on a floor pallet dozing, her face glistening with sweat from her hard labor. A deerskin blanket covered her and a red, wrinkled child, hardly bigger than a wildcat cub.

Anne and Richard named their son William. Richard made a cradle from a hollow log and traded furs for a child's Indian blanket. The blanket was as black as night, with a stripe as red as a male cardinal's feathers. Anne made a basket from the branches of a weeping willow tree. She wrapped William in the blanket and carried him with her when she worked in the fields and woods.

Every month, new people came to homestead near Anne and Richard. Land grew more expensive, so dozens of families ventured further west to stake a claim of land. Many of the homesteaders stopped for a meal and a night at Anne and Richard's small cabin. They talked of where game was scarce and where it was plentiful and of Indian troubles in the west. The Cherokee and Iroquois had signed a treaty giving up their claim to the Alleghenies. But the powerful Shawnee had not. Horrified once again at the invasion of their hunting grounds, the Shawnee and allied tribes launched new attacks on frontier settlements.

Visitors to Anne and Richard's cabins talked of how the Shawnee had scalped and killed Stephen Sewell, Felty Yoakum, and Archibald Clendenin. The Indians had taken their wives and children captive. Anne's face grew tight as she thought of the families' terrible fate. She worried about what the future would hold for her and Richard. If the Indians drove out the settlers in the Alleghenies, Anne and her neighbors would be next.

To help protect the frontier, Richard rode west to work again as a scout. Anne often stayed alone with William on their hilltop farm. She grew accustomed

Shortly after they were married, Richard Trotter continued his work as a scout, leaving Anne home alone with their newborn son.

to fending for herself. When the wild pear and redbud bloomed, Anne weeded corn. When blue jays screamed in paw paw thickets and snakes slithered through her kitchen garden, she hunted game. When the leaves turned scarlet and gold, Anne cut wood for winter, harvested corn, and picked sweet mountain huckleberries. With young William by her side, she traveled footpaths by sandy runs and watched golden "gabby birds" skim across the swift waters. Anne soon could read the forest floor as well as the circuit preacher who rode through each spring could read his black Bible. Paw prints, bent grass, broken branches—Anne knew how long it had been since a raccoon had passed, whether it was male or female, and where it was headed. Anne kept herself and William supplied with meat and enjoyed doing it. She felt good in the forest—as free as the wild things she tracked.

To ease the loneliness when Richard was gone, Anne sometimes visited Elizabeth Mann, a gaunt woman with gray hair and piercing eyes. She and her husband, Moses, owned a three-story mill sided with rough brown boards. Mann's Mill, the grandest structure for miles around, ground corn and wheat for settlers. Water flowed over a giant water-wheel that powered grinding stones inside. The mill towered above the creek in a clearing near the falls. Next to it sat an oblong house of mammoth-sized squared logs. A small log tavern and trading post stood nearby.

Similar to Anne's neighbors, Mrs. Mann had given birth to a dozen children, but not all survived. She and Anne talked of births and deaths, love and marriage, crops and livestock. Other women joined them, while their menfolk visited at the tavern. The men drank home-brewed ale and moonshine whiskey, debated county politics, and bet on fighting roosters. Over the years, Anne began to stand out as an unusual woman because sometimes she would join the men.

When Richard was home, he and Anne went together to the tavern. When he was gone, Anne went alone. Elizabeth Mann, who was like a second mother to William, gladly watched him when Anne asked. As time passed, Anne took to wearing one of Richard's fringed leather jackets over her dress. She wore a three-cornered felt hat on her head, with a thick brim to turn away sun and rain. In her belt she carried a tomahawk and knife. She rested a long musket rifle on her shoulder. At the tavern, Anne drank, laughed, and played cards.

Some settlers did not approve of Anne's "unlady-like" behavior and thought she was a bit "mad." They

This British cartoon commemorates the repeal of the Stamp Act in 1766.

believed God allowed men to do such things—but a woman's place was in the home. Others, such as her friends the Manns, accepted Anne as she was. The frontier had many colorful characters, and that made many backcountry people proud. The Eastern "Tuckahoes" could have all the social "dos and don'ts" they wanted. In the mountains, people lived as they wished. As for Anne, she never cared very much what others thought of her.

While Anne was learning to live life on her own terms and Richard was scouting, war brewed throughout the thirteen colonies. Rebellion brewed against

England to the east. Indians and white settlers battled to the west.

When Anne rode to Staunton for supplies, she had trouble paying the new taxes levied by King George III. The Stamp, Sugar, and Townsend Acts had forced colonists to pay special taxes on legal papers, newspapers, lead, glass, paint, and tea. The colonists struggled to tame and conquer a new land; then the King demanded they add their meager cash to his swelled coffers. Anne cursed a King who demanded much and offered nothing in return.

Even in Anne's remote corner of Virginia, people

Angry Bostonians dumped crates of English tea into Boston Harbor in defiance of unfair taxes.

followed the news from Boston, Philadelphia, Williamsburg, and London. At the local trading post and tavern, Anne and Richard learned that colonial leaders had complained to King George III about his unfair treatment. But the King had turned deaf ears to the protests.

In December 1773, Anne and her neighbors cheered when the Bostonians dumped English tea in the Boston harbor. The next spring, their cheers turned to prayers. To punish the rebellious colonists, the British Parliament closed the Boston Port and sent thousands of Redcoats to occupy the city. On a Sunday in June, Anne and other colonists attended Stone Church to pray for the deliverance of Bostonians and for the mother country to realize the error of its ways. To help the deliverance along, the Virginians heeded the Patriots' call to boycott British goods.

More well-off colonists stopped buying English tea and gave up using imported wool, silks, brocades, and cottons. Now when Anne rode to town, rich and poor, master and servant, Valley dweller and backwoods folks all dressed alike in suits made from rough homespun linen and wool.

Because Anne and Richard were not well off enough to buy English tea or silk, the boycotts meant little to them. It was land they and their kind craved, but it was land that the King and the Indians said they could not have. Richard Trotter and others had fought with the King's men to chase the French and Indians off the western land. Then the ungrateful King had forbidden colonists the right to push westward through the high mountains and into fertile valleys along and beyond the river the Indians called Spay-lay-wi-theepi, the wide and wild Ohio.

By 1774, Anne, Richard, and 30,000 other land-hungry settlers called the western mountains home, in defiance of the King and Indians. Some of the whites pushing deeper and deeper into the Indians' sacred hunting grounds admired Indian ways. They hoped to share the vast and fertile land. But many thought the only good Indian was a dead Indian. Among the land speculators and trappers were some bloodthirsty out-laws—brutal men escaping arrest back East for theft and murder. They feigned friendship with Indians, then slaughtered them. They also dressed as Indians and committed crimes against whites. Some stole horses, while others committed murder, scalping their victims so it seemed the Indians were to blame.

On a hot summer day, a group of white trappers and land-speculators invited a small Indian band camped near them to share their dinner. They pretended to be friendly, plied the braves with drink, then brutally murdered them all. Even Anne, who considered the Indians her enemies, was shocked to hear how the men had murdered the father, brother, pregnant sister, and other family members of the Mingo Chief Logan.

Logan was a highly respected Indian chief known for his kindness to whites and his great wisdom. He had been an advocate for peace. His family had always offered a friendly welcome to trappers, land speculators, settlers, and Indians from all tribes. Now Logan sought revenge. He vowed to take ten colonists' lives for each of his slain relatives. That summer, Logan took thirty scalps on the frontier.

Chapter Five

War in the East and West

Soon, full-scale border warfare erupted on the frontier. The royal governor of Virginia, the Earl of Dunmore, planned to converge with two armies on the Indian towns and lay waste to their fields. The governor himself would lead the royal army of British redcoats. This army would be joined by militia recruited from the area around Fort Pitt, where the Allegheny and Monongahela rivers rushed together to form the Ohio. Dunmore's army would travel down the Ohio River and meet the second army of Virginia recruits where the Great Kanawha joined the river at Point Pleasant. The merged forces would then march into Ohio Indian towns along the Scioto River and attack. Anne's husband, Richard Trotter, joined the frontier army.

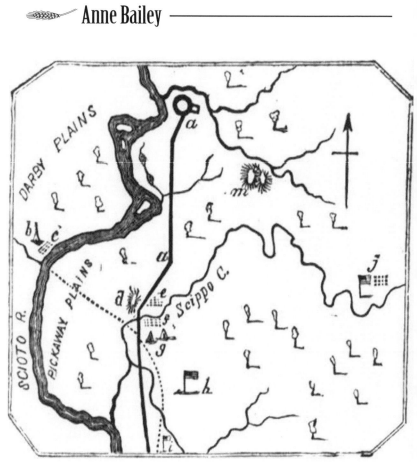

The Shawnee organized towns along the Scioto River.

Shawnee Chief Cornstalk knew the white army would be far stronger than the 800 Shawnee and their few hundred Mingo, Delaware, and Wyandot allies. The whites' guns were better, too. For generations, the Indian tribes had been pushed further and further west. Small pox and other diseases brought by Europeans had wiped out many as well. Cornstalk worried that war might destroy the Indian race once and for all. He worried about the future of his people and wished that whites and Indians could live together peacefully. With his sister, six-foot-tall Nonhelema, and his brother, Silverheels, Cornstalk struck out for Fort Pitt with the hope of peace.

Trading posts, taverns, stores, stables, blacksmith shops, a shipyard, and hundreds of tidy cabins surrounded the small log fort. Several thousand residents bustled about, helping to outfit the men gathering to make war against the Indians. As Cornstalk, Nonhelema, and Silverheels walked toward the quarters of the fort commander, Colonel Croghan, a crowd of angry men and women swarmed around them, shouting, pushing, and attacking.

The astonished trio stood back to back, knives in one hand and tomahawks in the other. They held off the angry throng for several minutes. When Croghan arrived, he fired his pistol into the air, breaking up the crowd. Silverheels had been badly wounded in the riot. For the chief of the Shawnees to be treated this way was too great an insult, and Croghan's apologies fell of deaf ears. With Cornstalk's hope for peace shattered, he and his group left for home. The Shawnee would join the Mingo Chief Logan, and the combined Indian army would drive the white settlers from western Virginia. At the council of war, Cornstalk told his painted braves: "If you must fight, you will fight; and I will see that you do fight!"

Meanwhile, in Lewisburg, Colonel Andrew Lewis had recruited his army of 1,100 western Virginians. Richard Trotter had said good-bye to Anne and William and left for Fort Union. It was not fondness for Governor Dunmore that made him join the frontier army. As royal governor, Dunmore was a hated man. He had taken away the right to assemble, punished protestors, and enforced British taxes. Richard knew Dunmore would jump at any chance to punish the rebellious colonists for their treasonous congresses, boycotts, and demonstrations of recent years.

Richard also had little respect for the British army that Dunmore was bringing into the mountains. Compared to the frontiersmen who had formed an army of proud citizens for home defense, the British soldiers received payment for their work. Yet distrust and dislike did not keep Richard and the other frontiersmen from heeding Dunmore's call for a massive Indian attack. Richard was willing to share a berth with the Redcoats if it could end the "Indian menace" once and for all. He joined the frontier army gathered in

Lewisburg and marched into the wilderness toward Point Pleasant.

For nineteen days, Richard and 1,100 Virginians marched through 160 miles of wilderness driving 108 cows for beef and 400 packhorses weighed down with 54,000 pounds of flour. An advance team slashed through the forest in front of them to make a road for the cavalcade of wagons, cattle, and soldiers. Richard prowled the surrounding forest with other buckskin-clad scouts. They watched for bands of hostile Indians that might try to waylay them. The Virginians marched down the Greenbrier, Bluestone, and Kanawha Rivers to the Ohio. Dunmore hoped the rugged terrain would cause many of the upstart western Virginians to desert. To make things even more difficult, several times he sent messengers with orders to change course. The Virginians suspected that Dunmore wanted to shame them. Either he wanted them to join the battle too late, or fight on their own.

Lord Dunmore was expected to boat down to Point Pleasant with a huge flotilla of rafts and canoes filled with 1,900 soldiers. But when Richard and his fellow soldiers reached the Ohio River on October 8, the Redcoats were nowhere to be seen. Richard and the other Virginians felt bitter and betrayed. They believed

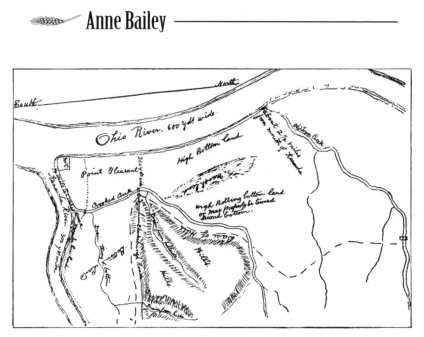

Point Pleasant, a peninsula on the Ohio River, was the location of a fierce battle between the American colonists and the Shawnee.

the governor was evading them on purpose, that Dunmore *wanted* them to fail in their war against the Indians. This would make the Virginians look weak—and make the Royal English troops look strong.

Soon Lewis received a message from Dunmore ordering the Virginians to travel upriver and join the northern army at Big Hockhocking River. Having enough of Dunmore's infuriating plans, Colonel Andrew Lewis ignored this order. His men were exhausted and needed rest. Also, moving north would take them further from the Ohio Indian towns. Richard Trotter helped pitch camp on the grassy peninsula of

Point Pleasant, collected saplings, and built pens for the cattle. Then he ate a scant meal of firecakes made from a mixture of cornmeal and water which was cooked on a hot rock. Just before nightfall, Richard gathered with the other men to hear Lewis bless their encampment. Lewis asked God to protect the men in battle.

Richard Trotter held his cap in his hands and bowed his head. As Lewis spoke, his mind filled with images of Anne and William waiting at home for his safe return.

The Virginians awaited word from Dunmore's army. The Virginians planned to march west to the Shawnee towns of Kispoko and Nonhelema's Town. But the warriors, Cornstalk, Logan, Red Eagle, and Black Snake, had other ideas. Cornstalk gathered with Indian leaders to form a battle plan. The Indian army would attack Lewis at Point Pleasant. "Now the seed of war has been planted and watered and already it sprouts. Whether it thrives and grows or is cut down remains yet to be seen," Cornstalk said.

On October 9, 1774, the 1,000 Indian braves, including the warrior squaw, Nonhelema, crossed the Ohio in bark canoes. As dawn broke, the largest army of Indians that had ever assembled on American soil attacked the frontier army from the rear. Scouts spread the word among the sleeping recruits that the Indians were attacking. The men scrambled from their blankets, grabbed their guns, and formed lines. Richard had missed being slaughtered in his sleep by a mere fifteen minutes.

The vicious battle lasted all day. First, the Indians forced the militia toward the river; then the militia forced the Indians deeper into the forest. Gun smoke was so thick, it blinded men on both sides. Screams, war cries, grunts, and groans pierced the air. Half-blinded, soldiers and braves fought in hand-to-hand combat until one killed the other and screamed out his triumph. Arrows and bullets flew through the smoke-filled air. Cornstalk walked up and down his line of warriors, shouting his encouragement: "Oui-shi-cat-to-oui! *Be strong*!" Silverhawk collapsed from exhaustion. Nonhelema carried him off the field to safety.

By nightfall, a fresh troop of 300 Virginians had arrived. Seventy-five Virginians and thirty-five Indians had died. Hundreds on both sides were wounded. The Indians withdrew across the Ohio to mourn their dead and treat their wounded. The next day, the blood-stained grass and forest floor was strewn with the weapons of the fallen. A crew combed the area, gathering twenty-three guns, twenty-seven tomahawks, eighty blankets, and many war clubs, shot-punches, and powder horns. The Virginians buried their dead. Among them was Anne's husband, Richard Trotter.

Chapter Six

Choosing a Westward Path

Anne did not learn of Richard's death at the Battle of Point Pleasant until late November. Returning soldiers visited Anne's remote cabin and gave her the sad news. They said that after the battle, the Virginians had marched toward the Indian towns, but Dunmore had stopped them. At Camp Charlotte, he had signed a peace treaty with the Indians. The only Indian leader not to attend the negotiations was Logan, who instead sent a message that brought tears to the eyes of whites and Indians alike. The message, repeated all over the colonies, read:

> I appeal to any white man to say if ever he entered
> Logan's cabin hungry, and he gave him not meat;
> if ever he came cold and naked, and he clothed

him not. During the course of the long and bloody war, Logan remained idle in his cabin, an advocate for peace. Such was my love for the whites, that my countrymen pointed as they passed and said, "Logan is the friend of white men." I had even thought to have lived with you but for the injuries of one man. Colonel Cresap, the last spring, in cold blood and unprovoked, murdered all the relations of Logan, not even sparing my women and children. There runs not a drop of my blood in the veins of any living creature. This called on me for revenge. I have sought it. I have killed many. I have fully glutted my vengeance. For my country, I rejoice at the beams of peace. But do not harbor a thought that mine is the joy of fear. Logan never felt fear. He will not turn on his heel to save his life. Who is there to mourn for Logan? Not one.

The soldiers told Anne the terms of the treaty. The Indians would share their hunting grounds in western Virginia and Kentucky, return white captives, and allow whites to travel the Ohio River in peace. In return, the whites promised not to attack Indian towns in Ohio. Logan's speech moved the soldiers, but not enough for them to agree with the treaty. We should have marched on the Indian towns and finished the job once and for all, they said with anger. Anne, stricken by grief, agreed. She cursed the Indians and cursed Dunmore. The messengers left, and Anne gave in to her grief. But Anne did more than cry over her husband's cruel death. She also went a little crazy.

First, Anne sent William, age seven, to stay at the Mann's. Then she stuffed some gear in a pack, grabbed her rifle, and mounted Liverpool. She rode through a light covering of snow to the cave behind Falling Springs Waterfall. There, she camped by an open fire, hunted for game, and let her hair hang loose and tangled. No one knew her whereabouts, and that was how Anne wanted it.

When they realized she had disappeared, the Manns went looking for her. They had no luck until Liverpool appeared without his rider. The Manns followed the horse's trail through the snow to the cave. There they found Anne half-frozen, half-starved, and crazed with grief. They brought Anne home to her cabin, where she rested and healed for the rest of the winter.

Meanwhile, war fever spread throughout the colonies. In May of 1774, George Washington and Samuel Adams met with leaders from all thirteen colonies in Williamsburg, Virginia. They decided to form a "Continental Congress" to meet in Philadelphia in Septem-

Samuel Adams helped to form the Continental Congress whose members demanded colonists' rights and would eventually sign the Declaration of Independence.

ber. The Congress would declare the colonists' rights to life, to liberty, to collect their own taxes, and to govern themselves. Then, in April of 1775, British Redcoats and colonial militiamen clashed in the battles of Lexington and Concord, Massachusetts.

Even as the first shots were fired, leaders and settlers debated whether to fight or to negotiate peace with Britain. Conservatives wanted to force the King to change his policies. Radicals wanted an independent nation. Colonists and Redcoats continued fighting on eastern battlefields. Yet it was not until two years later—July 4, 1776—that the second Continental Congress decided to issue the Declaration of Independence.

Back in Virginia, Anne emerged from her cabin in the spring of 1775. At the tavern and the trading post, the few Loyalists who dared to talk peace found themselves scolded by a fiery little woman with a thick Liverpool accent and a long musket rifle. Anne said that the King's agent, Lord Dunmore, had abandoned Richard and the Virginia militia at Point Pleasant when they made peace with the Indians. The King cared more for Indians and taxes than he did for the settlers who had tamed this wild land. Anyone who defended the King or the Indians was no friend of Anne's.

In March 1775, Anne cheered when she heard the stirring words of Patrick Henry: "Is life so dear or peace so sweet as to be purchased at the price of chains and slavery? Forbid it, Almighty God! I know not what course others may take; but as for me, give me liberty or give me death!" At the tavern, she listened eagerly when a man read aloud an exciting *Virginia Gazette* newspaper editorial, which declared: "The sword is drawn, and God knows when it will be sheathed."

Soldiers' wives were giving up their pewter to make bullets and sewing army coats from woolen blankets. Some wives followed the soldiers and worked for the

After Mingo Chief Logan avenged the murder of his family, he supported a peace treaty with the settlers.

army for half-pay. They nursed wounded soldiers and carried ammunition, beef, and coffee to soldiers in the field. Throughout the colonies, other women organized boycotts and signed petitions, or armed themselves with rifles, shovels, and brooms to waylay enemy messengers on isolated back roads. A few women disguised themselves as men and fought on battlefields as soldiers.

Many widows, such as Anne, tried to manage their homesteads, farms, and businesses alone. But without their husbands' labor and wages, many failed. Others sold themselves and their children as indentured servants, took in lodgers, or turned their homes into "ordinaries"—crude little taverns that offered nothing more than a meager meal and a corner to sleep in. Anne chose a different path.

Anne was tiny, but she was strong. She could ride and shoot better than many men. Restless and tired of the endless toil of managing a homestead alone, Anne longed to fight the battles of her time, and she craved both solitude and adventure. So she mounted Liverpool and rode west to take Richard's place, scouting in the war-torn wilderness.

In the late summer of 1775, Anne strapped a musket, axe, kettle, blanket, and powder horn on her black

The fiery words of Patrick Henry, "[G]ive me liberty, or give me death!" inspired Anne.

horse, Liverpool. She swung seven-year-old William onto the gelding's broad back. As dawn broke, they rode down the trace.

Overhanging branches of oaks, maples, and elms blocked out the sunlight and glistened with morning dew. Gold and scarlet leaves rained down onto a carpet of soft green moss, lacy ferns, and thorny Greenbrier vines. Under an ocean of leaves, giant grapevines roped from tree to tree.

Anne and William zigzagged past forty-foot boulders and tangled rhododendron thickets. The mountain stream rippled over flat rock shelves into cold, quiet pools. At Mann's Mill, Anne and William dismounted and walked to the big house, where Elizabeth waited in the doorway. Many of the older woman's family members had been killed in Indian raids, and she admired Anne's courage. She also loved William, whom she had known since he was born.

Anne explained to her friend what she felt she must do. She said goodbye to her young son. Then she turned, mounted her horse, and looked down at her son and friend standing in the doorway. Next year, William would go to school with the Mann boys at the new, one-room schoolhouse. At the prospering Mann homestead, William would eat from real pewter plates and go to sleep with a belly full of bread made from wheat, not corn. Anne would return during the winters to visit William.

Anne, no longer a girl at thirty-two years old, followed the Midland Trail, which had been hacked out by Richard and his fellow Virginia Regulars. She climbed the first Allegheny peak, which settlers called "breaking the backbone." She left behind her the fields she and Richard had worked so hard to grub. Perhaps their claim would soon be occupied by a homeless squatter. Or, their farm might become overgrown with weeds and saplings, a haven for deer and other small animals who no longer had to be afraid of Richard's hunting skill. Anne saw in the distance the long unbroken chain of the Allegheny mountains that looked like layers of worn blue velvet. She headed down into this wild land filled with giant trees, raging rivers, hostile Indians, isolated settlements, and primitive forts.

Anne worked as a frontier scout during and after the American Revolution. Spring through fall, she delivered guns, ammunition, food, and medical supplies between a string of wilderness forts set up to protect the settlers from British and Indian attacks. Winters, she returned to her cabin at Falling Springs to be with William.

Guided by a pocket compass, Anne rode along the high, rocky Allegheny ridges. Roots of young trees clutched rock crevices, as if frightened to let go. Tufts of mountain clover, bird's-foot violets, and ear-leafed magnolia trees filled the woods with honey-sweet smells. Whippoorwills sang, and otters slid down mud banks into rushing streams. Rivers roared and echoed as they tore through deep canyons.

Anne carved dugout canoes from tree trunks. On her knees, she paddled with quick sharp thrusts across swift, swollen rivers. Once across, she filled the canoe with heavy rocks and sank it to the bottom of a shallow, protected cove. When she needed to cross the rivers again, she plunged into the water, removed the rocks, and hauled the boat to the surface. Anne picked her way over woodland graveyards of fallen ancient trees, trudged through marshes, and scaled slippery shale hillsides. Rain made the creeks swell and the ground became slick and mucky. Clumps of mud clung to Liverpool's hoofs, making the going rough. Anne shared her woods with the hulking buffalo, the screeching red-tailed hawk, and the sly cougar that settlers called a "catamount."

Like other scouts, Anne learned to recognize the long scratch marks on tree bark made by "critters" standing on their hind legs, sharpening their claws. Anne walked softly and covered her tracks. She could throw a hunting knife at any mark. "I always carry an axe," she told those who asked how she managed on her own. "And I can chop as well as any a man."

Anne could load her musket on the run. First she would tear open one end of a paper cartridge with her teeth and sprinkle the gunpowder into the pan of the musket's firing mechanism. She then pushed the rest of the cartridge into the open end of the barrel, jamming the powder and bullet down with a steel

Anne became a scout during the Revolutionary War.

ramrod. The powder was set off by the spark that was created when the flint on the hammer struck the steel latch covering the pan. She could fire three or four shots a minute.

When the wind made trees crack like gunfire and sway like the sashaying skirts of dancing women, Anne huddled in the hollow trunks of sycamores. Mountain caves—cool in summer and warm in winter—also provided shelter. To protect herself from howling packs of wolves, she made blazing campfires. She built beds of sticks above the forest floor to protect herself from rattlesnakes and copperheads. Sometimes, Anne spread her blanket by the hearths of isolated settlers' cabins. But Anne found it hard to breathe when she was shut up inside, away from the fresh night air. So she ate a meal, shared a tale, and left to sleep in the stable straw, or under the familiar star-filled sky.

Back at Falling Springs, William worked in the mill with the Mann children. In a one-room school, he learned to read and write, which made Anne proud. Whenever Anne saw children on her travels, she thought of William and stopped to visit with them for a while. Anne taught children rhymes and prayers she had learned as a child in Liverpool. She showed them how to blow bubbles with the stalks of dried Joe Pye weed and how to make whistles from blades of grass. She imitated the animals and birds of the forest. When she screeched like a tree frog and bawled like a bullfrog, the children laughed and begged for more. "I saw an owl on the elm tree," she would say. Then cupping her hands before her lips, Anne would hoot like an owl.

During the Revolution, Anne's scouting services were desperately needed. Lord Dunmore and the other British generals had made allies of the Indians. The English promised to stop the colonists from taking Indian land. They offered the Indians money, guns, and liquor for the scalps of frontier settlers. Historians have called the Battle of Point Pleasant, where Richard died, "the opening act of the American Revolution." The frontier warfare was called the "Battle for the Back Door."

Anne, who was known as Anne Trotter now, arrived at the heavy wooden gates of the frontier forts dressed in mud-splattered men's clothing. Her hair tumbled down in a tangled mess from under her three-cornered hat. She was an odd sight, but the officer in command of the fort gratefully accepted her services. He gave her a few coins, fed her a meal, played her at cards, and gave her a dram of whiskey. Then he asked her to ride to another fort for needed powder, food, or medical supplies, or he asked her to carry a report or message to a distant officer.

There was a shortage of able-bodied men on the frontier, for most had marched 600 miles east to join General George Washington's troops. Or they had marched west across the Ohio River to attack and burn Indian villages, and take scalps of their own. Those who remained at the frontier forts were a motley crew of older men, women, children, and a handful of soldiers. Sometimes, when the British, or "Tories," and Indians threatened the forts, those inside trotted a few horses up and down wooden pallets to make it sound as if a large army was quartered there. When low on ammunition, they loaded their rifles with old nails, pieces of iron, and buckshot.

Riding stealthily through the woods, protecting the "back door," Anne kept an eye out for bands of Indians sent to raid isolated cabins and settlements. During the warm weather months, the Indians waited in the woods until the men had left a cabin to work in the fields. Then some of the Indians followed the men and ambushed them, while others broke down cabin doors and killed or captured the women and children. After they had killed their enemies, the Indians slashed off a strip of hair-covered scalp as a trophy. Women and children who were spared were taken captive and adopted into tribes to replace relatives who had been killed by whites.

Settlers built primitive log forts to protect themselves. When Anne warned settlers that Indians were near, they fled to these forts. Each fort had a courtyard surrounded by sharpened stake fences called "palisades." Anne scouted between a half-dozen western Virginia forts along the Midland Trail, from Staunton to Point Pleasant along the Ohio River. Riding from one fort to the next took at least a day. When the settlers deserted their cabins, the Indians burned them to ashes. The Indians also burned crops, making food scarce. Hunters had to slip away to look for game, then dash back before the gunfire attracted the Indians.

Anne once stopped at Fort Lee in Charleston, where the Elk River meets the Kanawha, when a large band of hostile Indians arrived and camped across the river. Fearing an attack, nearby settlers fled to the fort and prepared for a siege. Small children were shooed into lofts; men and women had their guns close at hand. Watchmen were posted. Then a man inspected the gunpowder barrel and discovered it was almost empty. Fear spread throughout the fort.

The able-bodied men were needed to defend the fort and could not be spared. Anne agreed to ride to Fort Union to get the needed gunpowder. The Fort was in Lewisburg, 100 miles away. Anne packed a sack with venison jerky and Johnnycake and covered herself in a dark cloak. At nightfall, she and jet-black Liverpool slipped out of the fort and into the woods. Anne stayed away from the main trail, where she might be detected. Anne and Liverpool galloped through dark woods and swam across the swollen rivers. After two days and a night of riding almost nonstop, she reached Lewisburg. Once there, she loaded gunpowder into sacks and rested briefly before returning. When she returned to Fort Lee, the settlers cheered as Anne arrived with the powder needed to stave off the Indian attack.

Anne's life was rough and rugged, but it suited her well.

Chapter Seven

After the War

In October 1781, Anne heard that the British had surrendered at Yorktown in eastern Virginia. The peace treaty declared that the Mississippi River was now the western boundary of the new "United States of America." But the Indians did not give up as quickly as the British, so Anne continued scouting until peace descended on the frontier in the mid-1790s. In 1785, she began scouting with a new companion.

At age forty-three, Anne married a fellow scout named John Bailey. Like Richard, John had fought at the Battle of Point Pleasant. Like Anne, he had scouted on the frontier ever since. John's doeskin jacket was worn gray with wear and stained dark with sweat. He smelled like woodsmoke, bear grease, and tobacco. He lived rough and played hard and found in Anne a companion to share the solitary life of a backwoods scout. Reverend James McCue, the first Presbyterian minister west of the Alleghenies, married them in a little log church.

After Independence, Indian raids continued in western Virginia. Richard and Anne scouted and carried messages and supplies between frontier forts. In the remote areas they traveled through, isolated settlers used mussel shell silverware and wooden plates. They ate what they could kill or gather in the woods and fled to the forts when Anne and John warned them that hostile Indians were near. Meanwhile, the once-sleepy frontier towns grew with each passing day.

In Lewisburg, the couple watched hordes of wealthy eastern "Tuckahoes" arrive to bathe in the healing mineral springs. The men wore ruffled shirts of fine linen, leather boots, spurs, and silk gloves. The women wore crepe dresses trimmed with yards of satin ribbons. The tourists danced at fancy balls and gambled. They believed the mountain spring water cured every ailment from "nerves" to rheumatism. People came in droves to bathe in log troughs filled with healing waters heated with white stones. They drank it, too, often laced with moonshine whiskey from local stills.

Anne and John often visited Fort Lee along the

The colonies declared independence from Great Britain on July 4, 1776.

Kanawha, where they mingled with a growing crowd of frontier riff-raff. A salt-mining industry boomed, and so did drunkenness, fighting, and gambling. Rough shacks lined the riverbanks for twelve miles. Overworked oxen and horses stood ankle-deep in mud, waiting to haul loads of red salt. Keelboats jammed the river. Anne and John danced to the lively tunes of fiddlers with the miners, loggers, and boat crews.

For ten years, Anne and John roamed the western Virginia mountains and boomtowns together before John Bailey contracted a sudden fever, which killed him. Anne, now in her fifties, buried her second husband on a high bluff overlooking the Kanawha River. Her wrinkled face and calloused hands looked brown and rough, like an old leather saddle. Twice widowed, Anne was now twice as tough as when Richard had died twenty years earlier. Not yet ready for the rocking chair, Anne Bailey murmured a prayer for John, then mounted her horse and continued rambling.

In Anne's twenty years of scouting, much had changed on the frontier. By 1795, the Indians had retreated beyond the Mississippi River. The forts became the homes of veteran officers. The men were home from war, and peace at last descended. Scouts were no longer needed in western Virginia. Anne's bones ached from hard riding and walking and outdoor living. But Anne applied mustard plasters to her joints to soothe them. She put a horse chestnut in her pocket to keep rheumatism at bay. Then she searched for work that would allow her to keep up her wandering.

The Alleghenies were still untamed, but the Midland Trail itself had become a busy highway linking small settlements and towns from Staunton to Point Pleasant. Farmers' homemade wagons pulled by oxen shared the road with brilliant blue Conestoga wagons pulled by a team of six or eight horses festooned with ribbons and jingling bells. Billowing white canvas covered the rounded frames that held westward-bound pioneers. Stagecoaches fought for space along the rutted road. The drivers hollered at passengers to lean out the window when the road curved to keep the coach from overturning. Also, the rivers were jammed. Giant flatboats brought streams of new immigrants headed for the wilds of Kentucky, Ohio, and the Carolinas. By the early 1800s, steamboats joined them—churning the water into great waves and filling the pure mountain air with black soot.

Anne joined a parade of immigrants, travelers, and drovers on the road. Sometimes on horseback and

Stagecoaches carried passengers into the American frontier after Independence.

sometimes on foot, she worked as a peddler. From back east, she fetched whatever her customers wanted and delivered the goods to their doors.

Unlike other peddlers, Anne left the main road to carry goods into remote areas. More and more settlers were staking claims in woodlands linked only by old Indian and buffalo trails. As a former scout, Anne knew the land well. As a one-woman delivery service, she was honest to a cent, yet shrewd. Her wartime cronies up and down the road greeted her with great affection. "What did you bring us Grandma?" excited children cried when they saw her coming.

In her pack, Anne always carried medicines to treat the sick, for doctors rarely ventured into the remote hills and hollers. Settlers made their own drops, teas, and plasters from herbs and flowers. They collected their own cobwebs for packing into bloody wounds. But they depended on Anne for more exotic cures, such as drops made from roasted hedgehog fat to cure deafness, or horrible-tasting bottled tonics brewed back east.

Anne kept housewives supplied with needles and pins. She sold James H. Hollaway of Point Pleasant his first pocketknife. She brought the first of Old Tommy Henning's handcrafted spinning wheels into the mountains. Waving a long stick, she sometimes drove herds of pigs, cattle, and even ducks to her customers. Captain William Clendenin, whose home was the old Fort Lee blockhouse, sent Anne to fetch the first tame geese to live in the Kanawha Valley. Clendenin was an old friend from her scouting days and just as shrewd as Anne.

"Anne, if you don't bring exactly twenty geese, I will not pay for any," he said, and Anne agreed. Then she drove twenty geese sixty miles to Clendenin's home. When she arrived, Anne told him one goose had died on the journey. "Well, Anne," the captain said gleefully. "You didn't bring the number named in the contract, and I cannot pay for them."

Anne walked out to where she had hitched her horse, took the dead goose from her bag, and threw it down in the yard. "There's your twenty," she said, with fire in her eyes. Captain Clendenin laughed and promptly paid up and invited Anne into the house for some venison stew.

Although Anne still preferred caves and trees to beds in houses, she often tarried at inns along the road. At Crow's Tavern and Frederick Gromer's Mill, she traded stories with other old-timers. Among them was Daniel Boone, another former scout who had become a state legislator and land surveyor after the war. Gromer was famous for the gunpowder mill he built in 1788. A woman and her son had gone to the mill in the dark, lit a candle, and blown the entire thing to bits. Both died, and the explosion shook the mountain. Gromer rebuilt the mill, but gave up making gunpowder and switched to grinding grain.

Anne was always welcome to a free meal at Richard Tyree's Long Ornery Inn in Lewisburg, which was 225 feet long and only thirty-five feet wide. Tyree would meet Anne at the door with a hearty handshake and welcome. Under the low rafters, a giant fire thawed her chilled bones, and hot cider warmed her insides. On the fire, a side of beef turned slowly on a spit. Above the flames sat a pan to catch its sizzling juices that would be made into hearty gravy for the evening meal. After eating, Anne would join the other guests who ranged from gentlemen and ladies to tradesmen and beggars. They gathered by the fire, tankards of ale in hand, sharing news of the weather, politics, land prices, and taxes. Often, Anne left afterward for her bower under the stars. But sometimes she treated herself to a comfortable night on a soft feather bed.

On her buying trips back in the Shenandoah Valley, Anne always stopped in at Callaghan's Inn. A red cow painted large as life hung above the inn's door. Callaghan got the idea for the sign from a play that poked fun at a bumbling English innkeeper. Sometimes Callaghan dressed like the innkeeper in the play. Anne roared with laughter as he swaggered about in breeches with knee buckles and a wing-tailed coat with buttons the size of pewter plates.

Anne also visited her son, William, on her trips back east. When he grew up, William married Mary Anne Cooper and became a justice of the peace. Around 1800, when he was in his early thirties, William moved with his family to a farm on the western shore of the

Ohio River. His home was across from Point Pleasant, where his father, Richard Trotter, had died in battle.

In 1818, Anne came to live near William and his family. Anne was seventy-six, but stubbornly refused to live in her son's spacious home. Instead, she built her own little log cabin nearby. Anne was a grandmother now. She could no longer mount a horse. Yet she did not stop rambling. In rain and shine, she walked or paddled her dugout canoe to visit old friends. On holidays, she marched in parades with militia units. With her, always, was her old musket.

One cool November night in 1825, Anne walked to her cabin with William's daughters, Phoebe, eight, and Jane, six. Anne was feeling bad, so she fetched her grandchildren to spend the night with her. The girls skipped along the path to the cabin, and Anne walked steadily behind. They built a fire in the hearth. As the night shadows gathered, the children sat curled at Anne's knee and begged for a story. As always, Anne obliged.

Anne told them of the time she came upon some Indians while riding her horse that she owned after Liverpool died. She named the horse Jennie Mann, after the daughter of her old friend, Elizabeth. Unable to outrun some Indians that were chasing her, Anne dismounted and scrambled into the underbrush. Then she crawled into a fallen hollow log. The Indians caught the horse and one of them sat on the log Anne was hiding in. But the Indian did not find Anne. Later, Anne followed their trail, and while they slept, she stole Jennie Mann back.

When Anne finished the story, Phoebe asked, "Grandma, did the Indians ever try to kill you?" Anne replied that the Indians thought the Great Spirit protected her, so they usually left her alone. Then Jane asked: "Were you afraid, grandma?" Anne replied that she had not been afraid. "I could only be killed, and everyone has to die sometime," she said.

Tired from a long day, Anne and her granddaughters laid down to sleep in Anne's bed. Later, Phoebe grew cold and woke, calling to her grandmother. Anne lay still and did not answer. Phoebe cried and Jane woke. They could not wake their grandmother, so they ran barefoot in their white shifts to get their parents.

Anne had died in her sleep at age eighty-three. Her family buried her in a pine box and marked the grave with a smooth, flat stone from the Ohio River. They grieved for her, but they knew Anne had no regrets. She left Liverpool, England, to become a servant in a distant colony. She left a servant's life to be a homesteader, wife, and widow. Sheleft a home, a son, and friends to lead a life of freedom, adventure, and service on the western frontier. She left the wilderness to spend her last days with the family she loved. Anne Hennis Trotter Bailey had led a good life, in a land worth calling home.

Appendix

"Mad Anne Bailey" Legends

As the name "Anne Bailey" spread through the new country, legends sprang up about her much like the legends and "tall tales" of Daniel Boone and Paul Bunyan. A few are recorded here.

As a child in England, Mad Anne was kidnapped on her way home from school. The thieves took her books to sell, then shipped Anne off to Virginia and sold her as an indentured servant. After years of worry and searching, her parents found out where she was. They came to the colonies to bring her home, but Anne refused to go. She preferred the American colonies to England.

Mad Anne followed Richard to Point Pleasant and witnessed his death. A strange, wild, savage spirit possessed her from that day on, and she swore she would have revenge for Richard's death by destroying the entire Indian race. She spoke languages fluently and told the Shawnee that the Great Spirit had given her magic powers. If they bothered her, she would have them swept from the face of the earth. This allowed her to attack Indians, but the Indians were usually too afraid to strike back. The Indians called Anne the "White Squaw of the Kanawha" and believed bullets could not kill her.

One day, a pack of ravenous wolves chased Anne through the forest. Just in time, she slipped through the gate of Fort Young. Anne dismounted, went into the blockhouse, and approached a group of soldiers sitting by the hearth. The men saw she had Indian scalps strapped to her belt, which was nothing unusual for Anne. But as she came closer to the light of the fire, the men gasped in alarm. Anne's face and body were covered with blood. It oozed from an ugly gash across her forehead, from ear to ear.

Someone brought Anne a big draught of whisky. She seized the cup and poured it down her throat, as if it were water and she was dying of thirst. Then, suddenly, she pulled from her chest two more Indian scalps. They were fresh and dripping with blood. "You call yourselves the lords of creation," she screeched at the men. "Beat that, you big, robust, blustering cowards!"

Mad Anne then took another swig of her drink and told her story. Riding through the forest, she had heard warnings from "the other world." Then something invisible touched her, and she knew that "danger was nigh." Anne rode on and came upon a band of three Indians who seemed friendly. But the spirit voice told her to kill the Indians or they would kill her. Anne answered the voice and killed all three. Two she killed by knocking their heads together. One she shot with her musket. The next day, she took the settlers to see the bodies.

When the Revolution broke out, Anne took breaks from scouting the wilderness and rode from town to town shaming men into joining George Washington's eastern army. She carried critical messages from Washington to his officers in the field, too. Often she joined the officers' contests of skills and could beat them in running, jumping, shooting, or hunting. She also would "swear like a trooper, drink whiskey like a bar-room lounger, and box with the skill of a pugilist." Once, when a young man spoke rudely to Anne, she threw him to the ground and then kissed him. The camp full of soldiers roared with laughter.

Some said Anne was a great beauty with streaming red hair. Others said she was a devout Christian who always carried a Bible and defended the helpless. She preached the word of God to settlers and spent Sundays rounding up children who played hooky from church. If a settler drank too much and mistreated his wife or children, Mad Anne shamed him into behaving. Later in life, Mad Anne taught school, and she lived to be 125 years old.

Appendix

Anne Bailey Poems

A Girl Scout of 1791

All day she braved the forest dark,
At night her bed the branches stark,
Nor quailed at e'en the wolf's wild bark: Anne Bailey.

Brave girl! Did bird nor beast affright,
Your only bed the mountain height,
Your only canopy the night: Anne Bailey.

And with the Pale Face beat that day,
Though only Men were in the fray,
Who really saved the country? Anne Bailey.

—Anne Shawkey, 1928

Anne Bailey

Settlers murdered in their beds
Others down the valley fled,
To where the Elk's bright crystal waves
Oh dark Kanawha's bosom lays
There safety sought and respite brief
In Fort Charleston Found relief
There they bravely met their woes
And kept at bay their Indian foes.

Camped over the river, under the western sky
The Indians' war-whoop, loud and high
Was answered by the panther's cry.
Homes and cabins blazing high
Crimson decked the midnight sky.

Days and weeks the warfare waged,
In fury still the conflict raged;
Still fierce and bitter grew the strife
Where every man he fought for life
Day by day the siege went on,
Till three long, weary weeks were gone

And then the mournful word was passed
That every day might be their last;
The word was whispered soft and slow,
The magazine was getting low.
They loaded rifles one by one
And then—the powder was all gone.

They stood like men in calm despair,
No friendly aid could reach them there,
Their doom was sealed, the scalping knife
And burning stake must end the strife.
One forlorn hope alone remained
That distant aid might yet be gained.
If trusty messenger should go
Through forest wild and savage foe,
And safely there should give report
And gunpowder bring from distant fort.

But who should go—the venture dare
The woodsmen shook in mute despair,
In vain the call to volunteer;
The bravest blanched with silent fear.
Each gloomy brow with labored breath,
Proclaimed the venture worse than death.

Each in terror stood amazed
And silent on the other gazed;
No word escaped—there fell no tear—
But all was hushed in mortal fear;
All hope of life at once had fled,
And filled each soul with nameless dread.

But one who stood amidst the rest
The bravest, fairest and the best
Of all that graced the cabin hall,
First broke the spell of terror's thrall.
Her step was firm, her features fine,
Of mortal woman the most divine;
But why describe her graces fair,
Her form, her face, her stately air?
Nay, hold! My pen, I will not dare!
T'was heaven's image mirrored there.

She spoke no word of fear or boast
But smiling, passed the sentry post.
And half in hope and half in fear,
She whispered in her husband's ear,
The sacrifice her soul would make,
her friends to save from brand and stake.

A noble charger standing nigh,
Of spirit fine and metal high,
Was saddled well and girded strong
With cord and loop and leather throng
For her led in haste from stall,
Upon whose life depended all.

Her friends she gave a parting brief,
No time was there for idle grief;
Her husband's hand a moment wrung,
Then lightly to the saddle sprung;
And followed by the prayers and tears,
The kindling hopes and boding fears
Of those who seemed the sport of fate,
Like birdling free on pinion light,
Commenced her long and weary flight.

The Indians saw the op'ning gate
And thought with victory elate
To rush within the portal rude
And in his dark and savage mood
To end the sanguinary strife
With tomahawk and scalping knife

But lo! a lady! fair and bright,
And seated on a charger light,
Bold and free as one immortal
Bounded o'er the op'ning portal.

Each savage paused in mute surprise,
And gazed with wonder-staring eyes.
A squaw! A squaw, the chieftain cries,
A squaw, a squaw, the host replies
Then order gave to cross the lawn
With lightning speed and catch the fawn

Her pathway up the valley led,
Like frightened deer the charger fled,
And urged along with whip and rein,
The quick pursuit was all in vain,
A hundred bended bows were sprung,
A thousand savage echoes run

But far too short the arrows fell
All harmless in the mountain dell
To horse, to horse, the chieftain cried,
They mount in haste and madly ride
Along the rough, uneven way
The pathway of the lady lay.

Though long and loud the savage yell
Re-echoed through the mountain fell.
She heeded not the dangers rife;
But rode as one who rides for life;
Still onward in her course, she bore
Along the dark Kanawha's shore
Through tangled wood and rocky way,
Nor paused to rest at close of day.
Like skimming cloud before the wind
Soon left the rabble far behind
From bended tree above the road
The flying charger wildly trode

In a steep and rocky gorge,
Along the rivers winding verge,
Just where the foaming torrent falls
Far down through adamantine walls.
And then comes circling round and round
As loathe to leave the enchanted ground
Just there a band of wand'ring braves
Had pitched their tents beside the waves.

The sun long since had sunk to rest
And long the light had faded west
When all were startled by the sound

Anne Bailey

Of howling wolf and courser's bound,
That onward came with fearful clang
Whose echoes round the mountain range

On through pathless wood
To swim the Gauley's swollen flood
To limb Mount Tompkins brow
Beyond the Hawk's Nest giddy height.
Like some weary, hunted dove
To the heights of Sewell Ridge.

And bravely rode the woman there,
Where few would venture, few would dare
And as the morning's sunbeams fall
O'ore hill and dale and forest hall
Far in the distance, dim and blue,
The friendly Fort arose to view,
Whose portal soon the woman gains
With slackened speed and loosened reins . . .

While justice on the scroll of fame
In letters bold, engraved her name
Anne Bailey: Pioneer Heroine of the Frontier.

—written by a Civil War soldier in 1861

Recommended Reading

Founding Mothers: Women of America in the Revolutionary Era. Houghton Mifflin, 1975.

Fritz, Jean. *Can't You Make Them Behave, King George?* Paperstar, 1996.

Fritz, Jean. *The Double Life of Pocahontas*. Putnam, 1983.

Furbee, Mary Rodd. *Outrageous Women of Colonial America*. John Wiley & Sons, 2001.

Furbee, Mary Rodd. *Women of the American Revolution*. San Diego, CA: Lucent Books, 1999. Oxford Univ. Press Children's Books, 1999.

Hakim, Joy. *From Colonies to Country* and *Making Thirteen Colonies* (History of United States, Books 1 & 2). New York: Oxford Univ. Press, Inc., 1998

Kamensky, Jane. *The Colonial Mosaic: American Women 1600-1760* (Young Oxford History of Women in the United States, Vol. 2). New York: Oxford Univ. Press, 1995.

Moody, James, *Myths of the Cherokee.* New York: Johnson Reprint Corp. [1970]

Bibliography

———•◆•———

Articles

Cole, Adelaide M. "Anne Bailey: Woman of Courage." *Daughters of the American Revolution Magazine* 114, no. 3 (1980): 322-325.

Cook, Roy Bird. "The Annals of Fort Lee." Charleston: *West Virginia Review* (1935.)

Hall, Grace M. "Under the Cover of Darkness." *West Virginia Review*, (June 1942): 155.

Kelle, Paul. "Historic Fort Loudoun." Vonore, TN: Fort Loudoun Association, 1958.

Leonard, Patrick J. "Anne Bailey: Mystery Woman Warrior of 1777." *Minerva: Quarterly Report on Women and the Military* 11, nos. 3-4 (1993): 1-4.

Books

Atkin, Edmond. *Indians of the Southern Colonial Frontier, The Appalachian Indian Frontier; the Edmond Atkin Report and Plan of 1755.* Edited with an introd. by Wilbur R. Jacobs. Lincoln: Univ. of NE Press, 1967.

Atkinson, George W. *History of Kanawha County.* Charleston: *WV Journal*, 1876.

Bailyn, Bernard. *The Peopling of British North America*: *An Introduction*. New York: Alfred A. Knopf, 1986.

Billings, Warren M. *The Old Dominion in the Seventeenth Century; A Documentary History of Virginia: 1607-1687.* Chapel Hill: Univ. of NC Press, 1975.

Blackwood, James R. *Tinkling Spring, Headwaters of Freedom: Protestantism and Liberty.* The Presbyterian Church in the United States, 1950.

Brooks, Geraldine, *Dames and Daughters of Colonial Days*. Salem: N. H. Ayer Co., 1984.

Cartmell, Thomas Kemp. *Shenandoah Valley Pioneers and Their Descendants.* Winchester, VA: Eddy Press Corp., 1909.

Conners, John A. *Shenandoah National Park: An Interpretive Guide*. Blacksburg, VA: McDonald & Woodward Pub. Co., 1988.

Craighead, James Geddes. *Scotch and Irish Seeds in American Soil: The Early History of the Scotch and Irish Churches, and Their Relations to the Presbyterian Church of America*. Philadelphia: Presbyterian Board of Publication, 1878.

De Hass, Wills. *History of the Early Settlement and Indian Wars of West Virginia*. Philadelphia: Wheeling, H. Hoblitzell, 1851.

Dexter, Elisabeth Anthony. *Colonial Women of Affairs*. Clifton, NJ: Augustus M. Kelley, 1972.

Dickson, R. J. *Ulster Immigration to Colonial America, 1718-1775*. Belfast: Ulster Historical Foundation, 1976.

Dodderidge, Joseph. *Notes on the Settlements and Indian Wars*. McClain Printing Company, 1824.

Ebersole, Gary L. *Captured by Texts: Puritan to Postmodern Images of Indian Captivity*. Charlottesville: Univ. Press of VA, 1995.

Egloff, Keith and Deborah Woodward. *First People, The Early Indians of Virgina*. Richmond, VA: The Virginia Department of Historic Resources, 1992.

Ellet, Elizabeth. *The Pioneer Women of the West*. Philadelphia: Henry T. Coates & Co., 1873.

Elstain, Jean Bethke. *Public Man, Private Woman: Women in Social and Political Thought*. Princeton Univ. Press, 1981.

Etienne, Mona, and Eleanor Leacock. *The American Revolution: Changing Perspectives*. Edited by William M. Fowler, Jr., and Wallace Coyle. Boston: Northeastern Univ. Press, 1979.

Evans, Sara M. *Born for Liberty: A History of Women in America*. New York: Macmillan/The Free Press, 1989.

Fischer, David Hackett. *Albion's Seed: Four British Folkways in America*. New York: Oxford Univ. Press, 1989.

Frost, John. *Pioneer Mothers of the West; or, Daring and Heroic Deeds of American Women*. Boston: Lee and Shepard, 1859.

Garland, Robert. *The Scotch-Irish: A Social History*. Chapel Hill: Univ. of NC Press, 1962.

Green, Harry Clinton and Mary Wolcott Green. *The Pioneer Mothers of America: A Record of the More Notable Women of the Early Days of the Country, and Particularly of the Colonial and Revolutionary Periods*. New York: Putnam's and Sons, 1912.

Hale, John P. *Trans-Allegheny Pioneers*. Cincinnati: The Graphic Press, 1886.

———— *History of the Great Kanawha Valley*. Madison, WI: Brant, Fuller and Co., 1891.

Hale, John S. *A Historical Atlas of Colonial Virginia*. Staunton, VA: Old Dominion Publications, 1978.

Harris, J.R. *Liverpool and Merseyside; Essays in the Economic and Social History of the Port and its Hinterland*. Edited by J. R. Harris. New York: A. M. Kelley, 1969.

Heatwole, Henry. *Guide to Shenandoah National Park and Skyline Drive*. Luray, VA: Shenandoah Natural History Association,1995.

Hennepin, Louis. *Women and Religion in America, Vol. 2*. Edited by Rosemary Radford Reuther and Rosemary Skinner Keller, San Francisco: Harper and Row, 1983.

Howe, Henry. *Historical Collections of Ohio*. Cincinnati: C. J. Krehbiel and Company, 1902.

Howison, Robert Reid. *A History of Virginia from its Discovery and Settlement by Europeans to the Present Time*. Philadelphia: Carey and Hart, 1846-48.

Hyde, Arnot. *Pictoral History of the New River: A Photographic Essay*. Charleston, WV: Cannon Graphics, 1991.

Hyde, Francis Edwin. *Liverpool and the Mersey: An Economic History of a Port, 1700-1970.* Newton Abbot, David and Charles, 1971.

Jackson, George Stuyvesant. *Uncommon Scold, The Story of Anne Royall.* Boston: B. Humphries, 1937.

Jennings, Francis. *The Ambiguous Iroquois Empire: The Covenant Chain Confederation of Indian Tribes with English Colonies from Its Beginnings to the Lancaster Treaty of 1744.* New York: Norton, 1984.

Johnson, Patricia Givens. *Irish Burks of Colonial Virginia and New River.* Blacksburg, VA: Walpa Pub. 1992.

————. *James Patton and the Appalachian Colonists.* Verona, VA: McClure, 1973.

————. *A History of Middle New River Settlements and Contiguous Territory.* Commonwealth Press, Inc., 1969.

Kegley, Mary B. and F. B. Kegley. *Early Adventurers on the Western Water.* Orange, VA: Green Publishers, 1980.

Kephart, Horace. *Our Southern Highlanders: A Narrative of Adventure in the Southern Appala chians and a Study of Life Among the Mountaineers.* Knoxville: Univ. of TN Press, 1976.

Kerber, Linda. *Women of the Republic: Intellect and Ideology in Revolutionary America*. Chapel Hill: Univ. of NC Press, 1980.

Kerby, Robert L. "The Other War in 1774: Dunmore's War." *West Virginia History*, 36(1): 1-16, 1974.

Kercheval, Samuel. *A History of the Valley of Virginia*. Woodstock, VA: J. Gatewood, printer, 1850.

Lewis, Virgil A. *Life and Times of Anne Bailey, the Pioneer Heroine of the Great Kanawha Valley*. Charleston, WV: Butler Printing Co. 1891.

Levy, Peter B. *100 Key Documents in American Democracy*. Westport, CN: Greenwood Press, 1994.

Lewis, Margaret. *The Common-place Book of Me: The Diary of Margaret Lynn Lewis*. Compiled by Mrs. William Roland Miller, Jr., and Mrs. James Clifton Wheat, Jr. National Society of the Colonial Dames in Virginia, 1976.

Lyman Chalkley. *Chronicles of the Scotch-Irish Settlement in Virginia, Vols. I, II, III*. Extracted from the Original Court Records of Augusta County, 1745-18, Rosslyn, VA, 1912-1913.

Mason, Augustus Luncy Mason. *Romance and Tragedy of Pioneer Life*. Cincinnati: Jones Brothers and Company, 1883.

McCartney, Grace Hall. "Anne Bailey in West Virginia Tradition." (Master's Thesis, Marshall College, August, 1954.)

McKnight, Charles. *Our Western Border, Its Life, Combats, Adventures, Forays, Massacres, Captivities, Scouts, Red Chiefs, Pioneer Women, One Hundred Years Ago.* Philadelphia: J. C. McCurdy & Co., 1875.

Mitchell, Robert D. *Commercialism and Frontier Perspectives on the Early Shenandoah Valley.* Charlottesville: Univ. of VA Press, 1977.

Nash, Gary B. *Red, White, and Black: The Peoples of Early America.* Englewood Cliffs, NJ: Prentice-Hall, 1982.

Nash, Roderick. *Wilderness and the American Mind.* New Haven, CN: Yale Univ. Press, 1982.

Noble, Allen G., ed. *To Build in a New Land: Ethnic Landscapes in North America.* Baltimore: Johns Hopkins Univ. Press, 1992.

Norton, Mary Beth. *Liberty's Daughters: The Revolutionary Experience of American Women, 1750-1800.* Boston: Little, Brown, 1980.

Porter, Sarah Harvey. *The Life and Times of Anne Royall.* Cedar Rapids, IA: The Torch Press Book Shop, 1909.

Rhys, Isaac. *The Transformation of Virginia: 1740-1790*. Chapel Hill: Univ. of NC Press, 1982.

Rice, Otis K. *History of the New River Gorge Area*. Montgomery, WV: West Virginia Institute of Technology, 1984.

Rouse, Parke. *The Great Wagon Road: From Philadelphia to the South*. New York: McGraw-Hill, 1973.

Rowland, Bessie James. *Anne Royall's USA*. New Brunswick, NJ: Rutgers Univ. Press, 1972.

Royall, Anne. *Sketches of History, Life and Manners in the United States*. New Haven: Printed for the author, 1826.

Ryan, Mary P. *Womanhood in America: From Colonial Times to the Present*. New York: New Viewpoints, 1979.

Schlissel, Lillian. *Women's Diaries of the Westward Journey*. New York: Schoken Books, 1982.

Seaver, James E. *A Narrative of the Life of Mrs. Mary Jemison*. Syracuse Univ. Press, 1990.

Simpson-Poffenbarger, Livia, ed. *Anne Bailey: Thrilling Adventures of the Heroine of the Kanawha Valley*. Point Preasant, WV: L. S. Poffenbarger, 1907.

Smith, Abbot Emerson. *Colonists in Bondage; White Servitude and Convict Labor in America, 1607-1776*. Chapel Hill: Univ. of NC Press, 1947.

Spruill, Julia Cherry. *Women's Life and Work in the Southern Colonies*. Chapel Hill: Univ. of NC Press, 1938.

Taylor, Colin F., and William C. Sturtevant. *The Native Americans: The Indigenous People of North America*. New York: Smithmark, 1996.

Thwaites, Reuben Gold, and Luise Phelps Kellogg, ed. *Documentary history of Dunmore's war, 1774*. From the Draper manuscripts in the library of the Wisconsin historical society and published at the charge of the Wisconsin society of the Sons of the American revolution. Madison, WI Historical Society, 1905.

Toner, J. M., ed., *Journal of My Journey Over the Mountains, 1747-1748, by George Washington*. Albany, NY: Joel Munsell's Sons, Publishers, 1892.

Trans-Allegheny Pioneers. Charleston, WV: Kanawha Valley Pub. Co., 1931.

Ulrich. *Good Wives*. New York: Oxford Univ. Press, 1970.

Washburn, Wilcomb E., ed. *The Garland Library of Narratives of North American Indian Captivities*.

New York: Garland Publishing Company, 1975.

Wilson, Howard McKnight. *Great Valley Patriots: Western Virginia in the Struggle for Liberty.* A Bicentennial Project Sponsored by Augusta County Historical Society, Staunton, VA. Verona, VA: McClure Press, 1976.

Wintz, William D. *Annals of the Great Kanawha.* Charleston, WV: Pictorial Histories, 1993.

Withers, Alexander Scott. *Chronicles of Border Warfare.* Clarksburg, VA: J. Israel, 1831.

Index